LEGENDARY GREEK NAMES

HERACLES
& HIS TWELVE LABOURS

JILL DUDLEY

PUT IT IN YOUR POCKET SERIES
ORPINGTON PUBLISHERS

Published by
Orpington Publishers

Cover design and origination by
Creeds, Bridport, Dorset
01308 423411

Printed and bound in the UK by
Creeds

© Jill Dudley 2023

ISBN: 978-0-9955781-5-9

HERACLES
HERO & DEMI-GOD

Zeus, supreme god of the heavens, knew that it was ordained there would one day be a great battle of the Gods and Giants. To help win it he was determined to conceive an exceptionally courageous hero who would help the gods overthrow the enemy. For the mother of his intended hero he chose the beautiful mortal woman Alcmena, wife of King Amphitryon of Tiryns in the Peloponnese. Zeus waited till the king was absent on some campaign and then, somewhat despicably, took on the guise of her husband. She, thinking her husband had returned early from battle, welcomed him to her bed. Later that same night King Amphitryon in person returned and went in to his wife who told him that he had already made love to her. Tiresias, a seer, pronounced the true facts and the king felt greatly honoured that his wife had been chosen by Zeus. The result of that night's double impregnation was the birth of twin boys to the queen.

Zeus' wife, the goddess Hera, was enraged by her husband's infidelity (something she frequently suffered), and did all she could to harm the babies. She sent a pair of serpents to kill them and, because one infant screamed at the sight of them, but the other seized and strangled them, it was immediately evident which was the son of Zeus, and which was not.

According to legend the Milky Way, that strange sweep of pale stars in the night sky, was caused by the infant Heracles. Apparently, Zeus laid the newborn infant at Hera's breast while she slept, but he sucked so strongly and so greedily, that Hera thrust him from her and her excess milk spurted across the sky, hence the Milky Way.

Heracles was educated by the best men of the day and became proficient in all the arts such as wrestling, archery, horsemanship, poetry and music. It is said, however, that he lacked musical ability and, when his tutor (the brother of Orpheus* the renowned singer and lyre player) criticised his ability on the lyre, Heracles in a rage hit him over the head with the instrument and killed him. He was accused of murder, but got off by saying he was justified because it had been in self-defence, which one of the judges of the dead in the underworld said was a non-indictable offence.

When the Battle of the Gods and Giants broke out Heracles, as his immortal father had foreseen, showed exceptional strength and valour. The giants used great boulders, whole trees and mountain peaks as missiles, but Heracles stood his ground and fired poisoned arrows at them, mortally wounding many. The giants, however, so long as they were on their own territory, remained immortal, so Heracles had to drag their bodies away from their home territory to die.

The goddess Hera remorselessly continued her jealous attacks on Heracles, irate that this prodigy of her husband Zeus had been born to a mere mortal and not to her, his true immortal wife. As part of her revenge, she rigged events in such a way that Heracles never succeeded to the kingdoms of Mycenae and Tiryns in the Argolid which Zeus had intended for him. Instead they became the realm of King Eurystheus whose wife bore him three sons.

Because Heracles had helped King Creon win back his kingdom of Thebes from the Minyans, Creon owed him a debt of gratitude and so gave Heracles his daughter Megara in marriage. They too had three sons. One day, when Heracles was in Thebes Hera, in one of her ruthless rages, struck him with a bout of madness during which Heracles, thinking his wife and sons were those of Eurystheus, murdered them. He would have killed his mother's husband also, had the goddess Athena not thrown a great rock at him and stunned him. When he came to his senses again, Heracles was horrified to see the dead bodies of his family, and to learn he was the one responsible for the carnage.

The story was poignantly told by Euripides in his tragedy *Madness of Heracles*. In it the distraught Heracles wanted only to die himself. His shame was magnified by the arrival of Theseus* (king of Athens) who, far from rejecting him and keeping aloof from the perpetrator of such a crime, persuaded him gently to accept his friendship and return with him to Athens where he would give him sanctuary.

In another story, after the murder of his family Heracles, overwhelmed with grief by what he had done, consulted the Delphic oracle to find out how to atone for the crime. The oracle told him he must first receive purification by serving as a slave to King Eurystheus for twelve years. It was during this period that Heracles was given his Twelve Labours, each one requiring superhuman effort, courage and fortitude. King Eurystheus clearly hoped Heracles would die in the attempt.

The first Labour of Heracles took place in the north-east of the Peloponnese and was commonly known as the Killing of the Nemean Lion. Though Heracles boldly confronted the lion, he was startled when he fired his poisoned arrows only to see they failed to penetrate its pelt, but fell uselessly to the ground. In dire peril, he hit it over the head with his olive-wood club and stunned it, then throttled it with his bare hands. Afterwards he used the lion's own razor-sharp claws to skin it, which is why from then on he was always seen wearing the lion-skin, not so much as a memento but for his own protection because it was impenetrable.

The second Labour was the killing of the Hydra of Lerna (near Argos in the Peloponnese) – a giant serpent with numerous heads that lurked in the marshes there. When one head was cut off others would grow. Heracles had to call in the help of his nephew Iolaus to cauterize each stump as he mutilated it. But it had an ally, a giant crab, which Heracles finally crushed under foot. He finally managed to cut off the last remaining head of the Hydra and buried it under a rock. The Hydra's blood was highly poisonous and Heracles stored it to use for his arrow-heads.

The third Labour was the catching of the Erymanthian Boar in a mountain of that name. It was to be caught alive, and to achieve this he drove it through a deep snowdrift till it was so exhausted Heracles was able to catch it in a net.

The fourth was the catching of the Hind of Ceryneia (about fifty miles from Mycenae in the Peloponnese). It was to be captured alive, and Heracles spent a year pursuing it before it finally surrendered.

The fifth was the destruction of the Stymphalian Birds

who were infesting the woods in Arcadia. Heracles scared them with a brass rattle and, as they soared into the heavens he killed many with his poisoned arrows, and the few that survived flew off never to return.

The sixth Labour was the Cleansing of King Augeas of Elis' Stables. These were located in the far west of the Peloponnese. It required Heracles to get rid of an accumulation of dung during the course of one day which was produced by the many herds of cattle that made use of the stables belonging to King Augeas. This arduous task Heracles achieved by diverting the nearby river Alpheus so its waters swept through the stables washing all the dung away.

The seventh concerned the Cretan Bull, either the one which brought Europa to Crete, or the bull who fathered the Minotaur. Heracles caught it alive and released it in Mycenae. It finally settled quietly in Marathon.

The eighth was to do with the Mares of Diomedes who belonged to a son of the god Ares and ate only human flesh. Heracles killed their owner and threw his body to the mares, whereupon they became tame and he brought them to Mycenae.

The ninth Labour was the stealing of the queen of the Amazon's girdle (named Hippolyte) which was coveted by King Eurystheus' daughter. It was taken by Heracles, either for the price of the Amazon's freedom, or from the queen's dead body.

The tenth Labour was the stealing of the Cattle of Geryon. To do this Heracles used Helios' golden bowl to reach Geryon's home. There he killed Geryon, his dog and his herdsman, then brought back the cattle to King Eurystheus.

The eleventh Labour concerned the Golden Apples of the Hesperides. For this Heracles enquired of Nereus (the Old Man of the sea) the way to the orchard of the Hesperides (the daughters of Atlas). There he slayed the dragon guarding the orchard and brought the apples back.

Finally, the twelfth Labour required Heracles to descend to the underworld of Hades to bring back Cerberus, the three-headed guard-dog at the entrance to the underworld. Its duty was to devour anyone attempting to escape. With the help of Hermes (a son of Zeus and messenger god of the Olympians) Hades, god of the underworld, finally agreed that Heracles could take Cerberus providing he returned him unharmed. Heracles picked up the monster of a dog and carried him back to King Eurystheus who, on seeing the loathsome creature, immediately jumped into a large brass tub where he always took refuge when frightened. Having completed this last Labour, Heracles carried Cerberus back to Hades as he had promised. From the spittle which fell from the jowls of Cerberus there grew the highly poisonous aconite plant.

Anyone might think that by the end of twelve Labours Heracles would be worn out after the strenuous efforts to fulfil them. But he had years more of life and even then, long before the famous Trojan War, there was enmity with the Trojans. Apparently, Heracles sailed against his foes with a fleet of eighteen ships. There he killed Laomedon, the father of King Priam whose son Paris was later to run off with the beautiful Helen* triggering the Trojan War.

After many more adventures, Heracles eventually died by means of a poisoned tunic. It was given him by his then wife,

Deianira, who possessed the blood of a centaur whose dying words had been to smeer the blood on one of his garments if ever she felt Heracles was losing interest in her – she did not know it was toxic, but thought it had magical qualities which would restore his love for her.

Once Heracles put on the poisoned tunic, however, the poison began its work, burning into his skin and leaving him in agony. Horrified by what she saw was happening to her beloved husband, Deianira hanged herself. It fulfilled a prophecy that Heracles would die, not at the hands of the living, but by one who was already dead.

In desperation Heracles sent an envoy to enquire of the Delphic oracle what he should do. The oracle's answer was that he should build his own pyre, climb on top and leave the rest to his father Zeus. This he did but, because he was lying on the top, no one could bear to be the person to set it alight. Eventually a Greek warrior named Philoctetes who happened to be passing, though some say it was his father, finally set fire to it. In return Heracles gave him his bow and poisoned arrows. This gift was later to help bring about victory to the Greeks in the Trojan War. (See Philoctetes in the Glossary).

As the flames mounted the pyre the mortal part of Heracles was burned away. There was then a great flash of lightning and Heracles was raised to join the gods on Mt. Olympus. It is believed that Hera at last accepted this divine hero, son of Zeus, and that he married Hera and Zeus' daughter Hebe, cup-bearer to the gods who was also associated with perpetual youth.

Denotes a separate booklet on the subject.

GLOSSARY

ADMETUS – King of Pherae in Thessaly, husband of Alcestis.

ALCESTIS – Wife of King Admetus of Pherae.

ALCMENA – Wife of King Amphitryon of Tiryns, and mother of Heracles by Zeus.

AMPHITRYON – King of Tiryns and husband of Alcmena.

ARES – God of war. Son of Zeus and Hera.

ARGONAUTS – The heroes who accompanied Jason in the ship Argo to recover the Golden Fleece.

ATHENA – Daughter of Zeus. She was goddess of arts, craft and weaving, and patron goddess of Athens. She was the embodiment of wisdom, and the owl was her symbol.

ATLAS – Son of the Titan Iapetus. He was given the task of holding the heavens on his shoulders for eternity as punishment for leading the Titans in the battle between the Titans and the gods.

CREON – King of Thebes, and father of Megara who married Heracles.

DEIANIRA – Last wife of Heracles.

DIONYSOS – God of wine and drama.

EURIPIDES – Greek dramatist 480-406 B.C.

EURYSTHEUS – King of the Argolid which included Mycenae and Tiryns. It was he who set his arch-enemy Heracles his Twelve Labours.

GIANTS – They were of human shape but with serpents' tails on their legs. They were born from Gaia (Mother Earth) when she was impregnated by the blood from Ouranos (Heaven) which dropped on her when their son Kronos (Time) castrated his father.

HERA – Wife and sister of Zeus, and goddess of women and marriage.

HERMES – Son of Zeus and the mortal woman Maia. He was messenger to the gods, and accompanied the souls of the dead to Hades.

- HELEN – Daughter of Zeus and Leda (wife of King Tyndareus of Sparta). She married Menelaus, but ran away with Prince Paris of Troy which triggered the Trojan War.
- JASON – Son of Aeson, the rightful king of Iolchos, whose throne was usurped by Pelias. The latter promised to give up the throne if Jason brought him back the Golden Fleece from Colchis.
- MEGARA – Daughter of Creon of Thebes. She was married to Heracles and they had three sons. Heracles murdered her and his sons when, in a fit of madness, mistaking them for the wife and sons of his arch-enemy Eurystheus.
- MENELAUS – King of Sparta, brother of King Agamemnon of Mycenae.
- ORPHEUS – Son of the Muse Calliope and possibly Apollo. He was a devotee of Dionysos. His singing was so divine that all were charmed by it.
- THESEUS – Legendary hero-king of Athens, the son of King Aegeus and Aithra (daughter of King Pittheus of Troezen).
- TIRESIAS – A blind seer from Thebes.
- TITANS – The offspring of the primeval Ouranos (Heavens) and Gaia (Mother Earth).
- ZEUS – Supreme god of the ancient world. He was married to Hera, but had numerous extra-marital affairs with mortal and immortal beauties, by whom he fathered many gods and demi-gods.

MORE FROM THE PUT IT IN YOUR POCKET SERIES:

GREEK MYTHS
THE JUDGEMENT OF PARIS
HELEN
KING AGAMEMNON
ACHILLES
THE WOODEN HORSE
ODYSSEUS

ISLANDS
CHIOS – HOMER
CRETE – THESEUS AND THE MINOTAUR
DELOS – BIRTHPLACE OF APOLLO
ITHAKA – ODYSSEUS
KOS – HIPPOCRATES AND ASCLEPIUS
LESBOS (MYTILENE) – SAPPHO AND ORPHEUS
NAXOS – THESEUS AND THE MINOTAUR
PATMOS – ST. JOHN THE THEOLOGIAN
RHODES – THE COLOSSUS
SAMOS – PYTHAGORAS AND THE HERAION
SANTORINI – THE LOST ISLAND OF ATLANTIS
TINOS – THE MIRACLE-WORKING ICON

SACRED SITES
ATHENS – THE ACROPOLIS
ELEUSIS – DEMETER AND KORE
EPIDAURUS – CENTRE OF HEALING
DELPHI – THE ORACLE OF APOLLO
CORINTH – ST. PAUL AND THE GODDESS OF LOVE
OLYMPIA – THE OLYMPIC GAMES

ALSO BY JILL DUDLEY:

YE GODS!
(TRAVELS IN GREECE)

YE GODS! II
(MORE TRAVELS IN GREECE)

HOLY SMOKE!
(TRAVELS IN TURKEY AND EGYPT)

GODS IN BRITAIN
(AN ISLAND ODYSSEY FROM PAGAN TO CHRISTIAN)

MORTALS AND IMMORTALS
(A SATIRICAL FANTASY & TRUE-IN-PARTS MEMOIR)

HOLY FIRE!
(TRAVELS IN THE HOLY LAND)

LAP OF THE GODS
(TRAVELS IN CRETE AND THE AEGEAN ISLANDS)

GODS & HEROES
(ON THE TRAIL OF THE ILIAD & THE ODYSSEY)

BEHIND THE MASKS
(IN THE FOOTSTEPS OF THE EARLY GREEK DRAMATISTS)

OH, SOCRATES!
(TRACKING THE LIFE AND DEATH OF SOCRATES)